A Letter From Liverpool

Written by Marie Hardy

Illustrated by Andy Rowland

Gran
8 Park Road
Belfast

Dear Gran,
How are you?

This week we visited Liverpool.
We went on the train.
It was fun!

Cam and I held hands to cross the street. There was lots of traffic.

We went up a steep hill to see the church.

When we were shopping, we
spotted a band singing in the
street. We had fun clapping to
the drum.

Cam got a little green lunch box
and I got some trainers.

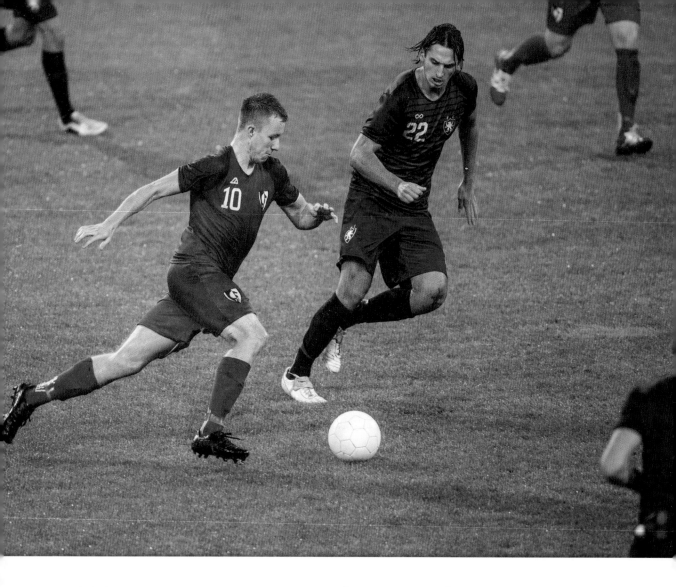

We went to see Liverpool against Everton. The men ran fast on the green grass.

The crowd sang and chanted.
I felt sad when it ended.

When it got dark, we went back
to the apartment.

Cam slept on the top bunk.
I slept on the bottom one.

We went out on a boat across the river. The air felt fresh.

We spotted a driftwood ship on
the sand. The flags were cool!

Then we sat down for a snack.
I had crisps and milk.
Crunch! Gulp!

Some of Cam's sandwich fell to
the sand. A gull took the crust!

What a thrilling weekend!
We said you must come on the
next trip. Hugs and kisses from
Amber, Cam, Mum and Dad.